Building History
EGYPTIAN PYRAMID

Gillian Clements

W
FRANKLIN WATTS
LONDON • SYDNEY

First Published in 2004 by
Franklin Watts
96 Leonard Street
London
EC2A 4XD

Franklin Watts Australia
45-51 Huntley Street
Alexandria
NSW 2015

Editors: Rachel Cooke and Sally Luck
Art Director: Jonathan Hair
Design: Mo Choy
Consultant: Dr Anne Millard

ISBN: 0 7496 5138 5

A CIP catalogue record for this book is
available from the British Library.

Printed in Malaysia

Contents

What are the pyramids?

The famous pyramids in Egypt are tombs built long ago for the great Egyptian kings – the pharaohs. They were made to house and protect the pharaohs' bodies and spirits after death.

The three pyramids at Giza, near Cairo, are one of the seven wonders of the ancient world.

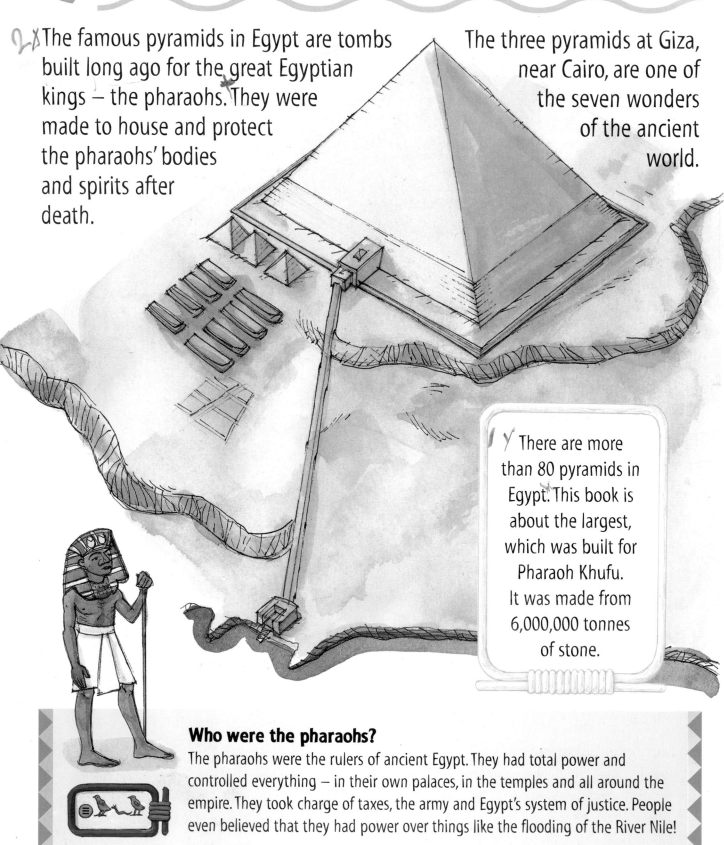

There are more than 80 pyramids in Egypt. This book is about the largest, which was built for Pharaoh Khufu. It was made from 6,000,000 tonnes of stone.

Who were the pharaohs?

The pharaohs were the rulers of ancient Egypt. They had total power and controlled everything – in their own palaces, in the temples and all around the empire. They took charge of taxes, the army and Egypt's system of justice. People even believed that they had power over things like the flooding of the River Nile!

c.5000BC
first Egyptian farmers

c.3000BC
first pharaoh

c.3100BC
first pyramid

c.2600–2500BC The Great Pyramids built
for Sneferu   Khufu   Khafre   Menkaure

Who was Pharaoh Khufu?

Pharaoh Khufu ruled Egypt
from around 2550BC. Ancient
Egyptians believed that, as
well as being a powerful ruler,
he was a living god. When it
was time for him to die, they
believed he would achieve
immortality and live forever
in the Afterlife.

Pharaoh Khufu ▶

When was Khufu's pyramid built?

The most famous pyramids were built in a
time we now call the Old Kingdom – from
around 2700 to 2100BC. Egyptians began
building Khufu's pyramid around 2550BC. It
took 23 years to complete.

Who built the pyramids?

The pyramids were designed
by skilled architects but
they were built by ordinary
Egyptians. Khufu's royal
architect, Nerfermaat, enlisted
huge numbers of farmers
and labourers to help the
expert craftsmen build the
giant tombs.

◀ Nerfermaat

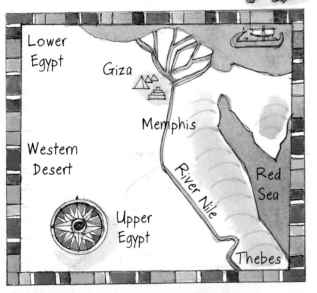

Lower
Egypt

Giza

Memphis

Western
Desert

River Nile

Red
Sea

Upper
Egypt

Thebes

Where was the pyramid built?

Khufu's pyramid was built on a dry rocky plateau near Giza,
above the River Nile's west bank. This was an ideal place for
a tomb complex. It was near to Memphis, the royal capital
of Egypt, and far enough from the Nile to avoid floods.

Why choose a pyramid shape?

Egyptian architects began to perfect the pyramid shape after about 2600BC. They knew that four triangular-shaped sides, rising from a square base, would make a very strong structure – strong enough to stand for all time. However, they also believed the pyramid was a sacred shape.

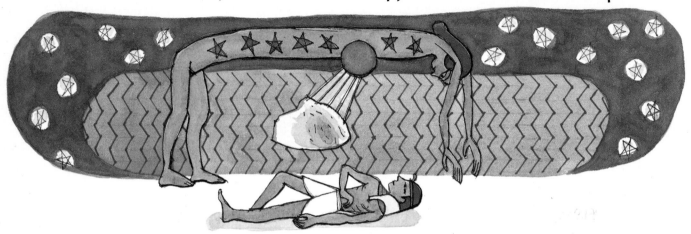

Why was a pyramid a sacred shape?

Ancient Egyptians believed that, when time began, a great ocean called Nun filled the Universe. Then a hill appeared in the ocean. The Egyptians called this pyramid-shaped mound a *ben-ben*. It was the first land to feel the Sun's rays and so they believed it must be a stairway to the sky, where Atum-Re the Sun God lived. Egyptians had many gods but Atum-Re was the first and the greatest.

Atum-Re's family tree

 Atum-Re – God of Sun and Creation

 Shu – God of Air

 Tefnut – Goddess of Moisture

 Geb – the Earth God

 Nut – the Sky Goddess

 Osiris – God of the Dead and Vegetation

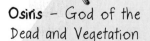 **Isis** – Goddess and Protector of Children

 Nepthys – Goddess of Women

 Seth – God of Desert and Storms

 Horus – falcon-headed Sky God

mastabas
c.3000–2000BC

step pyramids
c.2680BC

pyramids at Meidum
design evolves
c.2613–2589BC

The Bent Pyramid

The Red Pyramid

Did the Egyptians always build pyramids?

The ancient Egyptians hadn't always built pyramids. Ordinary Egyptians were laid to rest in sand graves. Earlier pharaohs had been buried under simple box-shaped tombs called mastabas, which were made from mud bricks. As the Egyptian architects became more skilled, these mastabas grew bigger and more complicated. Eventually they became a copy of the sacred mound shape – the stairway to everlasting life. The great pyramid tomb had finally been perfected.

Why use this shape for a tomb?

Egyptians believed that the pyramid would be the pharaoh's tomb forever. They therefore made sure it could withstand the Sun, wind and sand of the scorching desert, as well as protect the pharaoh and his treasure from grave robbers. To do this, builders created passages and chambers deep inside and beneath the pyramid. These would protect the pharaoh's carefully preserved body and soul.

For the first stepped pyramids, mastabas were placed on top of one another, making them look like stairways to heaven. Later, the Egyptians made the pyramids smooth-sided. They believed this would help the pharaoh's spirit launch itself directly at the Sun!

Who were the ancient Egyptians?

The all-powerful pharaoh ruled over the Egyptian people, through a very organised system of class and status. The system was not unlike a pyramid in shape.

10

Pharaoh Khufu Egyptians believed that Pharaoh Khufu kept a sort of 'cosmic' order and could, for example, control the rise and fall of the River Nile.

The pharaoh's family The pharaoh's sons worked for him at court. One of them, usually the son of his chief queen, would rule after him.

Egypt's noble families These rich families owned great estates and acted as local rulers. They paid scribes to carry out the work of administration in their own area.

Priests White-robed priests performed rituals in the temples. They had to wash many times a day, and shave their heads and bodies to make themselves pure enough. The junior priests taught, copied texts and learnt how to read the sky to make accurate calendars.

Scribes Scribes were the backbone of Egyptian society, because they could read and write. They were the civil servants who ran everything from the temple offices to the farms and even the army. Without scribes, the pharaoh's government would not have worked.

The army Egypt was so strong during the Old Kingdom period that it only needed a small regular army. The soldiers protected trade and dealt with border raids.

Craftworkers, builders and skilled men These people were often the servants of nobles or administrators. They could read and write just enough to do their work properly.

Farming people Most ancient Egyptians were farmers who could neither read nor write. They generally worked on the rich Black Land left by the Nile floods each year. They lived in simple mud houses, grew crops and kept animals.

Slaves and captives Most slaves were captured enemies who were prisoners of war. Some were Egyptians who had sold themselves into slavery to escape debt.

Where were the pyramids built?

The Egyptians chose the sites for their pyramids with great care. If they built too close to the Nile, the pyramids' foundations would shift and become flooded. They would also take up valuable farming land.

Where was Khufu's pyramid built?

Khufu's pyramid was built on a firm limestone cliff at Giza, away from the Nile floods, but close to royal Memphis where Lower Egypt's delta land meets Upper Egypt. Giza was not just the site of Khufu's pyramid — it was actually a tomb complex. The Egyptians built other tombs there for lesser royals and for nobles. Later, two more pyramids, for Pharaohs Khafre and Menkaure, and three small 'Queen' pyramids for Menkaure's female relatives, were added.

① **the Giza tomb complex**
Khufu's, Khafre's and Menkaure's pyramids, and the Queen pyramids.

② **Saqqara**
Pharaoh Djoser's step pyramid and the surrounding burial complex.

③ **farm villages**
Clusters of mud-brick houses where people and animals lived side by side. Found all along the Nile.

④ **Abydos**
Traditional burial place of the god Osiris and of Egypt's first pharaoh.

⑤ **Valley of the Kings**
After the pyramid era, Egyptians buried their pharaohs in the Valley of the Kings.

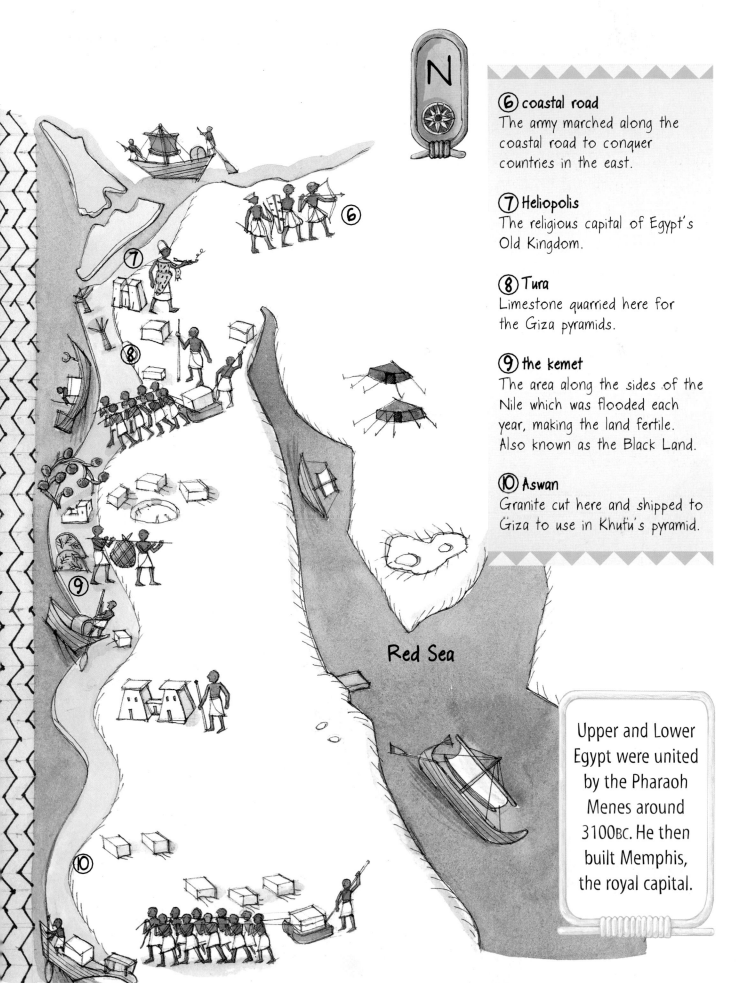

⑥ coastal road
The army marched along the coastal road to conquer countries in the east.

⑦ Heliopolis
The religious capital of Egypt's Old Kingdom.

⑧ Tura
Limestone quarried here for the Giza pyramids.

⑨ the kemet
The area along the sides of the Nile which was flooded each year, making the land fertile. Also known as the Black Land.

⑩ Aswan
Granite cut here and shipped to Giza to use in Khufu's pyramid.

Red Sea

Upper and Lower Egypt were united by the Pharaoh Menes around 3100BC. He then built Memphis, the royal capital.

How was the site laid out?

All ancient Egyptian royal burials were in the Western Desert. People saw the Sun set in the west every night, and so they linked the west with the Kingdom of the Dead – the home of the chief underworld god Osiris.

Apart from the pyramid, what other buildings were there?

Nerfermaat's plans for the site included the pyramid itself and a mortuary temple close by. A causeway would then link them both to a valley temple on the bank of the Nile. The temples were beautiful buildings with pillars and many rooms, rather like palaces.

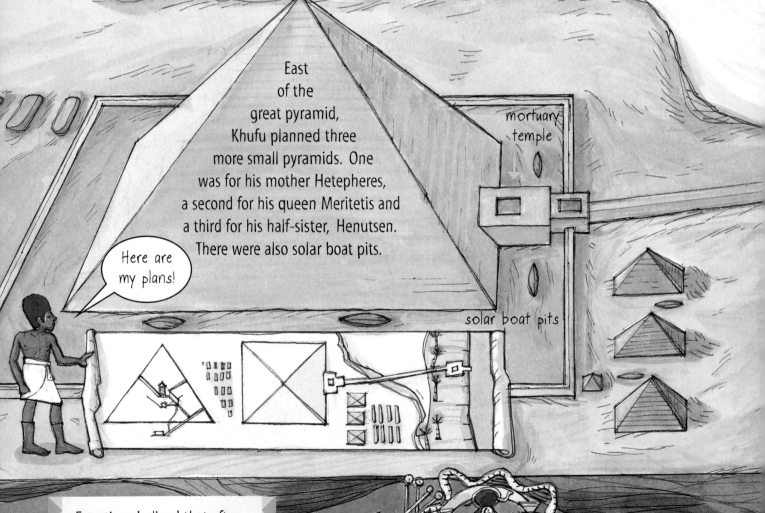

East of the great pyramid, Khufu planned three more small pyramids. One was for his mother Hetepheres, a second for his queen Meritetis and a third for his half-sister, Henutsen. There were also solar boat pits.

Here are my plans!

mortuary temple

solar boat pits

Egyptians belived that after the Sun set in the west, it continued to sail on through the night, underground.

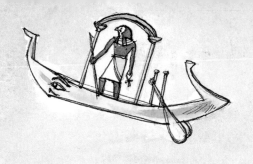

What were the solar boat pits?

Each day when the Sun god Atum-Re sailed across the heavens, he ensured that the seasons —and night and day — were kept in balance. Khufu was thought to be a son of Atum-Re. Egyptians believed that, in the Afterlife, he would also need a solar boat to sail across the heavens beside his father, so they buried some in pits around his tomb.

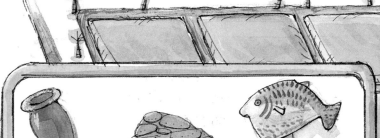

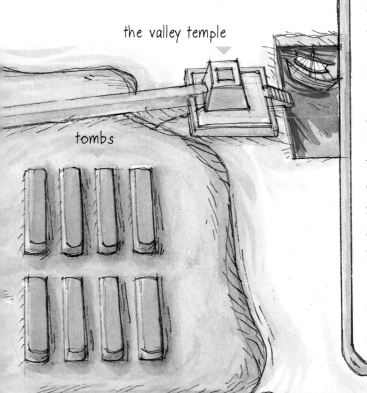

the valley temple

tombs

What have archaeologists found at Giza?

Archaeologists have discovered the causeway, temples and other tombs near Khufu's pyramid, as well as many small objects. These finds tell us a lot about how the pyramid builders lived and worked. In the remains of a workers' village found south of Giza, archaeologists discovered fish and many animal bones, bread ovens and cooking pots. This tells us that the workers were well-fed. Then, in a nearby cemetery, archaeologists found that labourers and skilled workmen had been given their own mastabas and miniature pyramid tombs. This shows that they were given respectable burials.

Pictured as a red disc on a boat, the Sun was carried through the watery chaos of the underworld, ready to rise again in the east the next morning.

Who built the pyramids?

More than 20,000 men were involved in the building of Pharaoh Khufu's pyramid. These men were expected to labour from sunrise to sunset, in the name of the Pharaoh.

How did Pharaoh Khufu find 20,000 builders?

The labourers who helped make Khufu's pyramid were not trained builders. They were ordinary people who were ordered to leave their farms and work on the burial site. Their labour was a sort of tax claimed by the Pharaoh: a tax paid in muscle-power, not money. The men toiled from July to November, when the Nile was in flood. They then returned to their farms when the waters receded. These labourers felt honoured to be asked to work for the Pharaoh.

Labourers were put into work gangs of about 20 men. These gangs gave themselves names, like 'Followers'. One gang left some graffiti in Khufu's burial chamber!

stonemasons at work

Which building skills were used?

Some labourers worked in the quarries. Others built and hauled stones. Skilled men were needed too, and Nefermaat selected the best trained stoneworkers. These experts had to cut and shape millions of limestone blocks that would be used to build the pyramid. Scribes were also needed. They marked and numbered the stones to make sure each was taken to the correct place on the pyramid. Many important skills were required, including mortar-making, carpentry and metalwork. Boatmen were also needed to transport the huge stone blocks from the quarries down river to the pyramid site.

It took 200 men to haul just one granite block. They weighed 50 tonnes each!

These are the workers who built my tomb.

scribe mortar-maker mason

carpenter metalworkers

stonecutter surveyor foreman

How were the pyramids built?

Khufu inspected the rocky pyramid site when labourers began to lay down the first stone blocks, but this was not the beginning. Much preparation had already been done.

What were the first steps?

Before building began, the vital first step was to find true north. Egyptian astronomers knew the night sky very well. They found true north by standing in the centre of a circle and tracing the passage of a star from east to west. Armed with this knowledge, the surveyors accurately marked out the northern, southern, western and eastern sides of the pyramid's base. The labourers then levelled the land in between.

Racking stones

Casing stones

Core stones

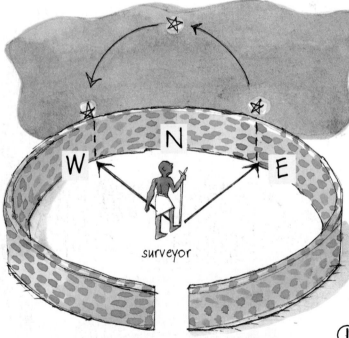

surveyor

In all, there were to be 200 layers, or courses, of stone.

How did the workmen level the site?

It was crucial to have a flat foundation, if the pyramid was to be solid enough to stand for eternity. Historians are not quite sure how it was done, but many think that the builders cut channels and filled them with water.

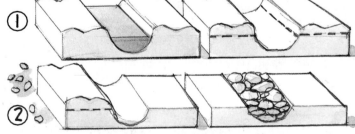

① Water finds a level in the rock channels.

② Labourers cut the rock down to this level and fill in the holes to make a flat site.

Quarry men cut out stone blocks.

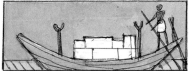

Boatmen carry the blocks to the pyramid site.

Gangs of workmen haul the stones along the causeway to the pyramid.

How did the building begin?

When the pyramid's base was marked and levelled, teams began to lay down the solid limestone floor.

We compete with rival gangs to be the best stone-haulers!

They worked from the outside through to the centre, where they dug a shaft for the first of the pyramid's three burial chambers.

We cut the stones into perfect shapes!

They then laid out the first course of the pyramid's tough granite blocks. Granite would be used to protect the outside of the first 15 of the pyramid's 200 courses.

I'm the foreman. I make sure the work gangs do what I tell them!

19

How were the blocks raised?

No one knows for sure how the Egyptians raised the stone blocks. One ancient Greek traveller suggested they used a lifting machine, but few believe that now. Most archaeologists believe the Egyptians built ramps.

The Egyptians used ramps made of river-mud, rubble, logs and mortar. Each ramp rested on the pyramid 'steps' as it grew. However, no one is sure if there was one big ramp or several smaller ones.

one large single ramp

a combination of the two designs, currently favoured by most archaeologists

many spiral ramps

What was inside the pyramid?

From the outside, the pyramid looked solid. However, the architect Nefermaat had made plans for three chambers inside, as well as connecting passages and four vents, pointing to important stars.

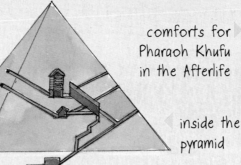

inside the pyramid

comforts for Pharaoh Khufu in the Afterlife

Khufu's chosen burial chamber would hold his possessions when he was dead. They would be the everyday things he needed in the Afterlife. The chamber also held a large granite coffin called a sarcophagus.

Portcullis doors made of heavy granite slid in vertical grooves cut in the passage wall. These doorways were made to protect the tomb from robbers.

◀ sarcophagus

How did the team build the main chamber?

All these internal pyramids were lined with granite. They were built at the same time as its outer structure. The construction involved careful planning, to ensure each chamber and passage came together in the right place. Great technical skill was also needed to get the angles of the passageways and vents correct.

The Egyptians realised that the pyramid would be extremely heavy, so they made five roofs for the chamber. The top roof was especially strong.

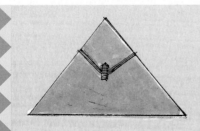

What were the vents used for?

Egyptians believed that these vents were direct routes to the sky. By reciting a special spell, Khufu's spirit would open the copper-handled doors in the vent, leaving his soul free to reach the heavens.

How was the pyramid finished?

The huge stone structure had towered over the Nile Valley for more than 20 years. Now at last it was time to finish the pyramid and place the final stone block – the capstone.

How did they fit the capstone?

The teams landed the capstone from a Nile river-boat. They hauled it to the pyramid's base, and then up a ramp to the very top of the pyramid. As the builders fitted it into place, exactly over the centre of the pyramid's base, priests chanted prayers and burned incense.

Chanting priests followed as the capstone was dragged to the top of the pyramid.

What were the finishing touches?

As the builders descended from the top, they stripped away the remaining ramps and fitted the pyramid's limestone casing. The limestone was polished with abrasive powder. Finished at last, the smooth, white pyramid gleamed in the Egyptian desert.

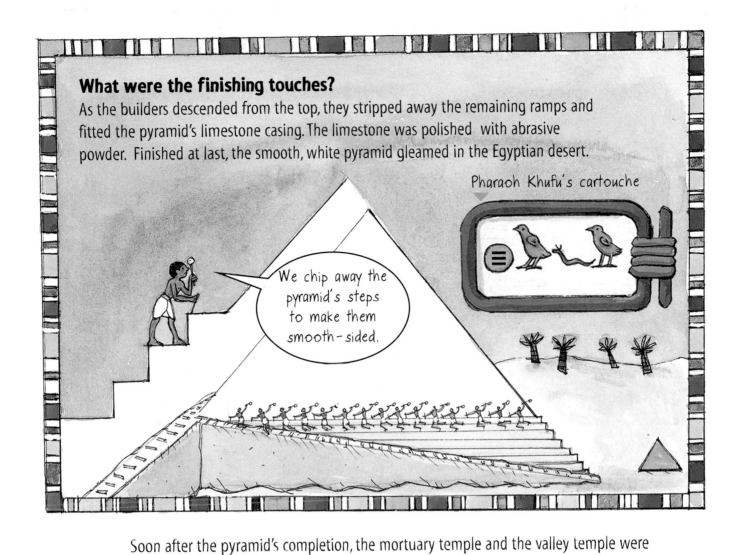

Pharaoh Khufu's cartouche

Soon after the pyramid's completion, the mortuary temple and the valley temple were finished too. The causeway was covered over and decorated, and labourers dug seven pits by the pyramid to hold Khufu's boats. In the Afterlife he would need them to sail across the heavens like his father, Atum-Re, or for sailing down the Nile. One of the boats would have been used to transport Khufu's coffin to Giza, after he died.

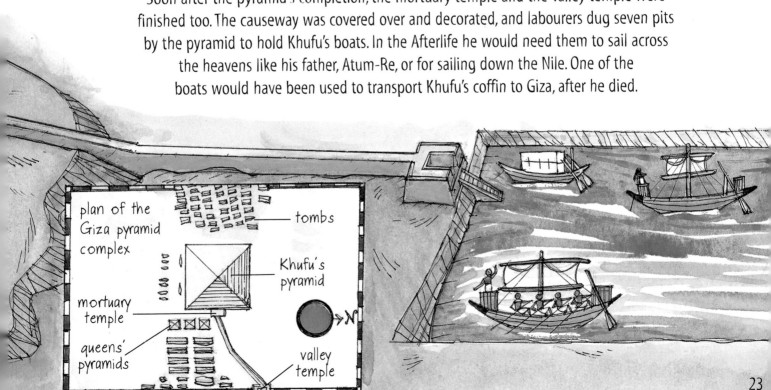

What happened when Khufu died?

When Khufu died, everyone began to prepare for his last journey – his journey to the pyramid and the Afterlife.

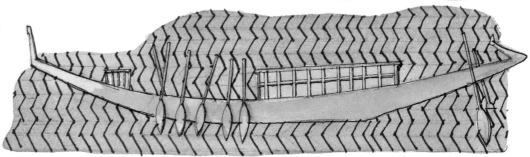

A royal barge carried Khufu's body along the Nile. When it arrived in Giza, mourners carried his coffin to the valley temple. Egyptians believed that as they entered the temple, their king was passing through the doors of heaven.

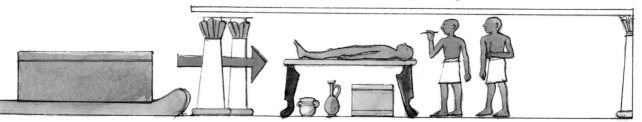

Embalmers prepared Khufu's body for his life after death, in a process called mummification.

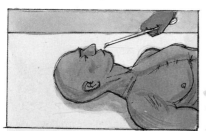

The process began by hooking the brain out through his nose.

They then cut through his side to pull out the liver, lungs, stomach and intestines.

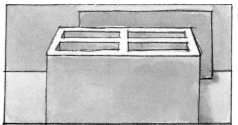

They stored these in a special canopic casket, but left the heart inside his body.

Next, the body was washed and packed in natron. Natron was a salt collected from a desert lake.

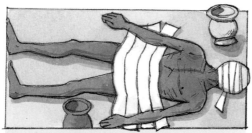

When the natron had dried out the body, embalmers coated it with oils and resins. To finish, they bandaged the body with many layers of linen strips, tucking pieces of gold leaf and precious items in between.

They then applied a final coat of resin.

After the final coat of resin, they painted a face over the bandages.

A ceremony called the 'Opening of the Mouth' took place in the hall of the valley temple. Priests performed special rituals to give the mummified pharaoh back his senses and make him live forever in the Afterlife.

◀ the ba

How did Khufu enter the Afterlife?

Ancient Egyptians believed everyone had a ka and a ba. Ka was a person's soul, or spirit. Ba was their spark of life. Egyptians imagined it as a bird. When people like Pharaoh Khufu died, Egyptians believed that the ba flew from his body. Then, when it flew back to him in the pyramid, he would live forever.

Why was mummification so important?

Mummification was important because the Pharaoh's ba had to recognise its own preserved body, especially the face and head. If it could not recognise its body, it would not be able to re-unite with it in the pyramid and give the Pharaoh his eternal life.

the ka

sarcophagus

Where was Khufu finally laid to rest?

Khufu was finally laid to rest in the pyramid's topmost chamber. The priests placed his coffin in a granite sarcophagus, and left his canopic casket nearby. The chamber was filled with other items he would need on his journey. When they left, the priests sealed the tomb and the pyramid's passageways. They hoped they were sealing them forever. Only Khufu should now pass through the granite doors between the worlds of the living and the dead.

canopic casket ◀

What happened to the pyramids?

Egypt's pyramids were built to last forever. They have stood for 4,500 years. What have they seen in that time?

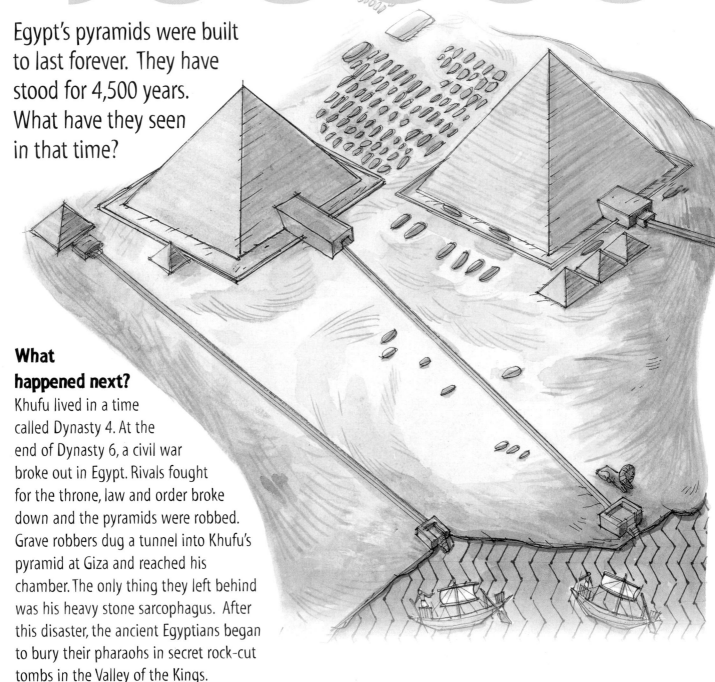

What happened next?

Khufu lived in a time called Dynasty 4. At the end of Dynasty 6, a civil war broke out in Egypt. Rivals fought for the throne, law and order broke down and the pyramids were robbed. Grave robbers dug a tunnel into Khufu's pyramid at Giza and reached his chamber. The only thing they left behind was his heavy stone sarcophagus. After this disaster, the ancient Egyptians began to bury their pharaohs in secret rock-cut tombs in the Valley of the Kings.

Robbers began to loot pyramids from around 2150BC

Who visited Egypt in the past?

Egypt's magnificent pyramids have attracted famous visitors for hundreds of years, for example Herodotus from ancient Greece. Napoleon is another famous visitor. He invaded Egypt in 1799 and his French army discovered the Rosetta Stone. This stone was inscribed with Greek and Egyptian writing. When scholars translated its strange hieroglyphics, we were finally able to read about, and understand, Egypt's ancient pyramids and its people.

Herodotus c.485 – 425BC

Napoleon 1769 – 1821

How did tourism grow?

As travel links improved, more and more people visited the pyramids. By the late 19th century, tour operator Thomas Cook was offering cruises down the Nile. In 1922, archaeologists discovered the golden treasures of Tutankhamen's tomb in the Valley of the Kings. This attracted even more visitors than before.

Tutankhamen's death mask

This graffiti was found inside Khufu's tomb. It had been written by a gang of workmen.

Who visits Egypt today?

Today Egypt's capital city, Cairo, stands next to Khufu's pyramid and tourists still flock to marvel at the ancient buildings. Archaeologists continue to work on the site and, with the help of developing technology, they are still making new discoveries about life in ancient Egypt.

Timeline

 c.5000BC Farming is already established in Egypt.

 c.3500sBC Egyptians have invented an early form of hieroglyphs.

 c.3100sBC Upper and Lower Egypt unite. The new royal capital of Memphis is built during the rule of King Menes.

 c.2650BC The Old Kingdom begins.

 c.2650BC Pharaoh Djoser's architect builds the first step pyramid at Saqqara.

 c.2500sBC The Great Pyramids and the Sphinx are built at Giza.

 c.2500BC Atum-Re, the Sun god, is Egypt's most important god.

 c.2150BC The Old Kingdom ends in chaos. Pyramids and tombs are looted.

 c.2100BC–c.2000BC Thebes becomes an important centre in Egypt.

 c.2040–1650BC The Middle Kingdom period.

 c.1650BC Eastern invaders conquer north Egypt in horse-drawn chariots.

 c.1570BC–c.1070BC The New Kingdom. Egypt builds its empire.

 c.1479–c.1457BC First female Pharaoh. Pharaohs are now buried in the Valley of the Kings.

 c.1400BC Huge temples built in Egypt.

 c.1347BC–c.1338BC Tutankhamen rules.

 c.1100BC More royal and noble tombs are looted.

 c.600BC Greek influence in Egypt spreads with merchants, travellers and mercenary soldiers.

 332BC Alexander the Great conquers Egypt.

 305BC Alexander's general Ptolemy becomes King Ptolemy I of Egypt.

 196BC Rosetta Stone was made.

 51–30BC Rule of Cleopatra IV. The Romans then defeated her and took Egypt into the Roman Empire.

28

Glossary

archaeologist
A person who digs up and studies the remains of buildings and objects from the past to find out about the people who made them.

architect
A person who designs buildings.

capstone
The final stone to be placed on top of an Egyptian pyramid.

causeway
A raised path or road.

embalmers
People who prepared dead bodies for the Afterlife, using various herbs and salts. The process was called mummification.

foundations
The base on which a building is constructed.

granite
A very hard rock, often used for building.

hieroglyphics
The picture writing used in ancient Egypt.

mastaba
A box-shaped tomb made from mud bricks or stone.

mortar
A cement-like mixture used in building, to hold stones and bricks together.

mummification
The preservation of a body after death.

quarries
Places where large amounts of stone are dug from the ground, usually to use in buildings.

ramp
A sloping surface which runs from one level to another.

sarcophagus
A stone coffin.

scribe
In the past a scribe was a person who could read and write, and was employed to use these skills.

tax
The money or goods which people paid to their government or their ruler.

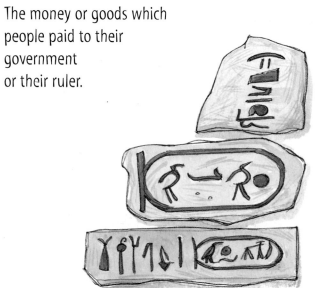

Index